Body  Books

Get a Move On!

Anita Ganeri

Evans

Evans Brothers Limited

Published by Evans Brothers Limited
2A Portman Mansions
Chiltern Street
London W1U 6NR

© Evans Brothers Limited 2003

First published 2003
Printed in Hong Kong by Wing King Tong Co. Ltd

British Library Cataloguing in Publication Data
Ganeri, Anita
  Get a move on!. - (Body books)
  1. Human locomotion - Juvenile literature
  2. Human physiology -
Juvenile literature
  I.Title

ISBN 0 237 52400 7

CREDITS

Editor: Louise John
Design: Mark Holt
Artworks: Julian Baker
Production: Jenny Mulvanny
Consultant: Dr M Turner
Photographs: Steve Shott

ACKNOWLEDGEMENTS

The author and publisher would like to thank the following for kind permission to reproduce photographs:

Science Photo Library, p12 (Professors P. Motta/ Department of Anatomy/University 'La Sapienza', Rome), p13 (Department of Clinical Radiology, Salisbury District Hospital), p15 (Astrid and Hanns-Frieder Michler), p22 (Philippe Plailly/Eurelios).

Photograph on p11 by Peter Millard. All other commissioned photography by Steve Shott.
Models from Truly Scrumptious Ltd.
With thanks to: Nicole Arellano, Nicola and Justin Mooi, Mylton Burden, Indiana Frankham, Ariadne Snowden, Courtney Thomas and also Ellen and Jack Millard.

VISIT OUR WEBSITE
www.evansbooks.co.uk
Evans

Contents

What makes you move?

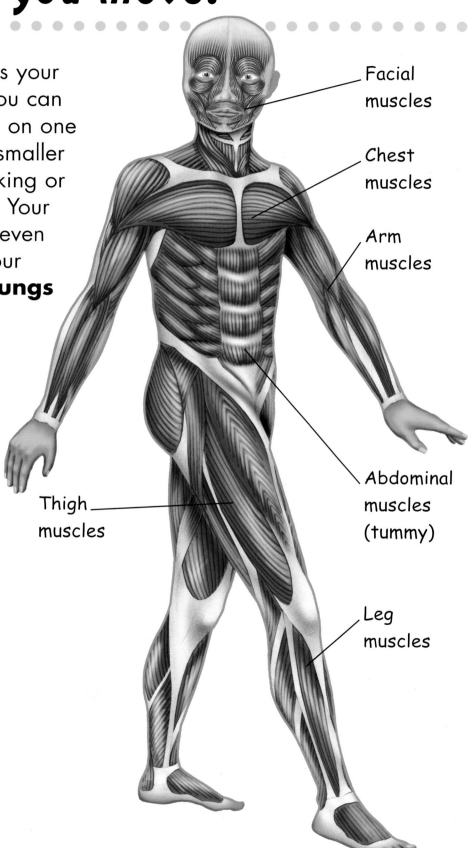

Facial muscles

Chest muscles

Arm muscles

Abdominal muscles (tummy)

Leg muscles

Thigh muscles

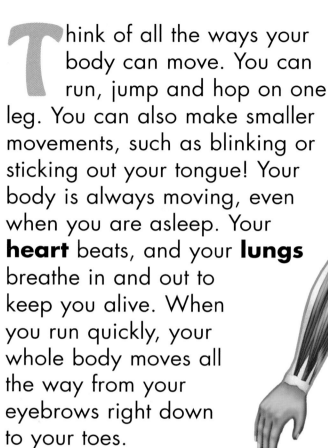

Think of all the ways your body can move. You can run, jump and hop on one leg. You can also make smaller movements, such as blinking or sticking out your tongue! Your body is always moving, even when you are asleep. Your **heart** beats, and your **lungs** breathe in and out to keep you alive. When you run quickly, your whole body moves all the way from your eyebrows right down to your toes.

AMAZING!

You have about 640 muscles in your body. They make up about a third of your body weight.

You are able to move because of the way your muscles, bones, brain and nerves all work together. Some muscles make you move by pulling on your bones. They move parts of your body, such as your arms and legs. Other muscles, such as those in your face, pull on your skin to make you smile or frown.

LOOK AT ME! ◎ LOOK AT ME! ◎ LOOK AT ME! ◎ LOOK AT ME! ◎ LOOK AT ME! ◎

Muscles make your eyes look at the words and pictures as you read a book. You also use lots of muscles to turn over the page.

Your skeleton

There are more than 200 bones inside your body. They make up your bony skeleton. When you were born, you had about 350 bones. But some of the smaller bones joined together as you were growing up. Your bones are all different sizes and shapes – long, short, round and flat. Each bone has its own special name.

AMAZING!

Your biggest, longest and strongest bone is the bone in the top of your legs. It is called your femur.

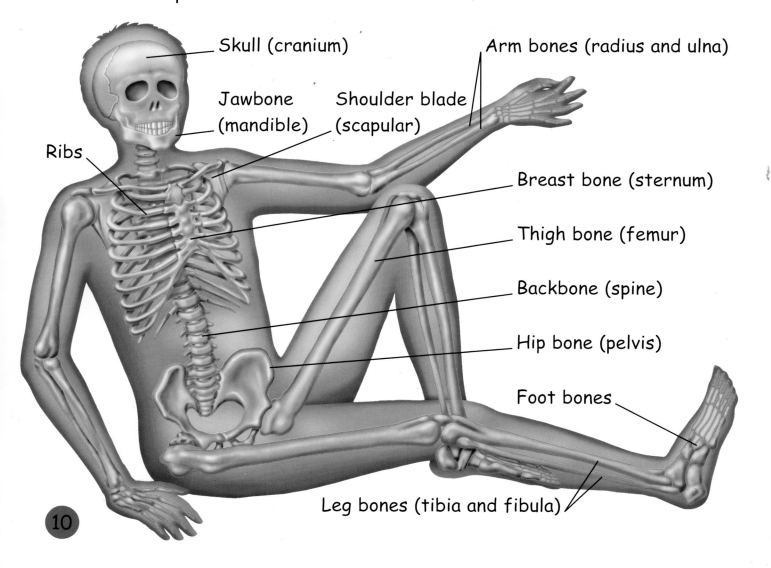

Skull (cranium)

Arm bones (radius and ulna)

Jawbone (mandible)

Shoulder blade (scapular)

Ribs

Breast bone (sternum)

Thigh bone (femur)

Backbone (spine)

Hip bone (pelvis)

Foot bones

Leg bones (tibia and fibula)

Your skeleton is very useful. It holds your body up and gives you your shape. Without your skeleton, your body would collapse in a crumpled heap. Your skeleton is very strong. It protects the soft parts of your body from being bashed or knocked. For example, your skull protects your delicate brain and your ribs protect your heart and lungs. Your skeleton also helps you move. Your bones work with your muscles to make you get a move on.

LOOK AT ME! LOOK AT ME! LOOK AT ME! LOOK AT ME! LOOK AT ME!

As your bones grow, you grow taller. How tall are you now? Can you guess how tall you'll be when you are grown up?

11

What's inside a bone?

Your bones are mostly made from water and a hard, stony stuff called **calcium**. A bone is quite stiff but can bend too so that it does not snap. The outside of a bone is very hard. But the inside is soft and spongy. This makes bones very tough and strong, but also very light. A special skin covers the whole bone. Some bones have jelly inside them. This is called bone marrow. It makes new red blood **cells** for your body.

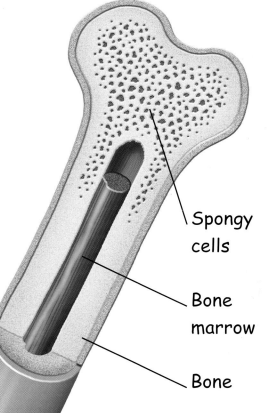

AMAZING!

The smallest bones in your body are hidden deep inside your ears. They are only the size of grains of rice. They help you to hear.

Spongy cells

Bone marrow

Bone

Bone marrow shown under a microscope.

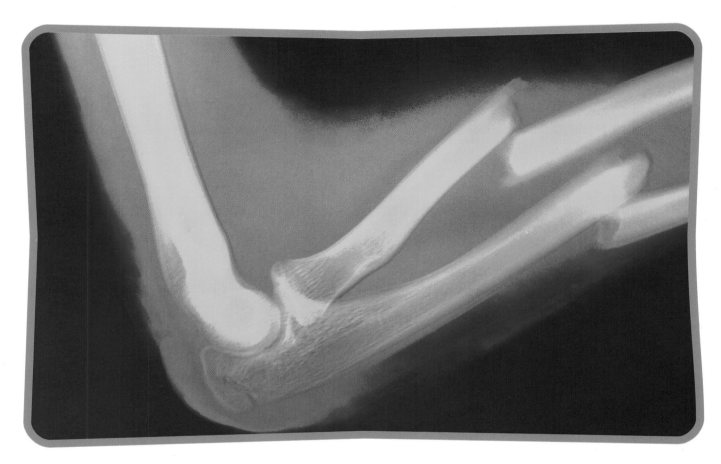

An x-ray of a badly broken arm.

If you break a bone, it can mend itself. But it often needs help from a plaster cast to make sure the broken ends mend properly. Doctors use special photographs called **x-rays** to look at your skeleton to see if a bone is broken. Your bones show up clearly in the picture.

LOOK AT ME! LOOK AT ME! LOOK AT ME! LOOK AT ME!

Gently press your knee, your elbow or your chin. Can you feel something hard and knobbly under your skin? These are some of your brilliant bones.

Moving bones

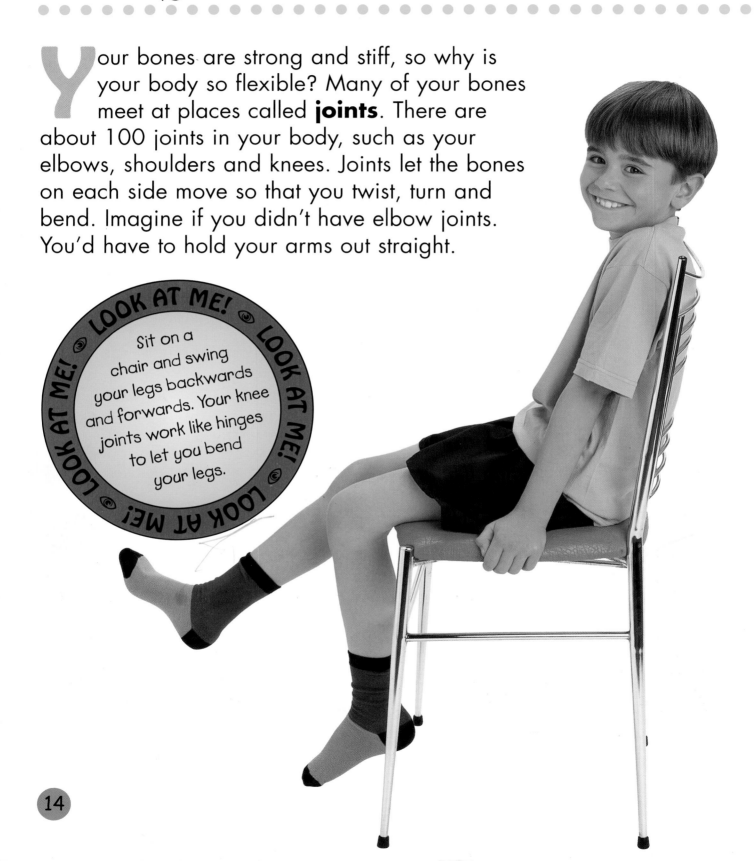

Your bones are strong and stiff, so why is your body so flexible? Many of your bones meet at places called **joints**. There are about 100 joints in your body, such as your elbows, shoulders and knees. Joints let the bones on each side move so that you twist, turn and bend. Imagine if you didn't have elbow joints. You'd have to hold your arms out straight.

LOOK AT ME!

Sit on a chair and swing your legs backwards and forwards. Your knee joints work like hinges to let you bend your legs.

The bones in a joint don't usually touch. The ends of the bones are covered in pads of soft gristle, which stops the bones from rubbing together. A special liquid keeps the joint slippery and well-oiled. The bones in a joint are held in place by strong, stretchy straps, called **ligaments**.

Some of your joints, like your elbows and knees, work like door hinges. But others, like your hip, are ball-and-socket joints, Your hip joint lets your leg swing round.

A picture of a hip joint – a ball-and-socket joint.

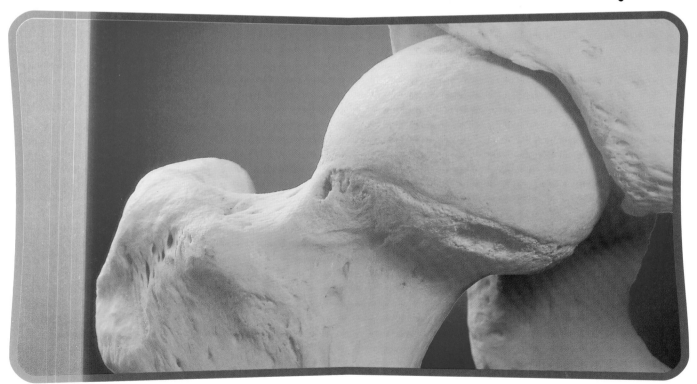

15

Heads and tails

Your skull is a hollow, bony case sitting on top of your neck. One of your skull's main jobs is to protect your delicate brain. The bones in your skull are joined together like a jigsaw. When you were born, your skull was soft and squashy. This helped you to squeeze out of your mother's body. As you got older, your skull turned into hard, strong bone.

LOOK AT ME! Have a good yawn! Which part of your skull is moving? The only part that moves is your jawbone. This allows you to bite, chew, talk and yawn.

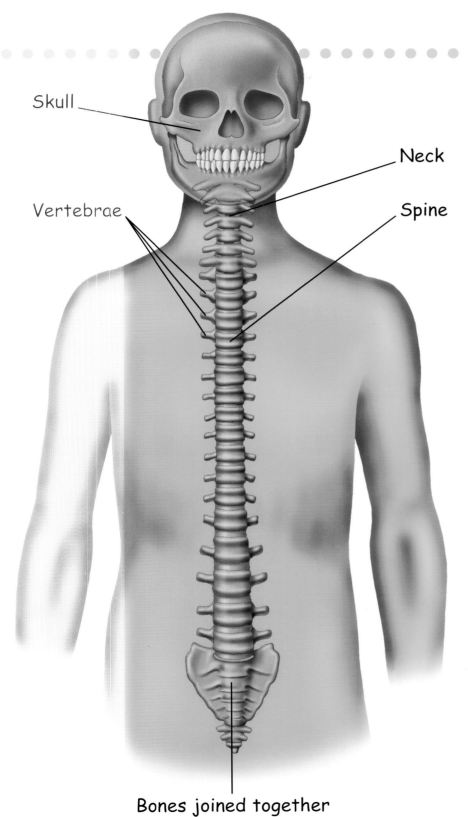

Skull

Vertebrae

Neck

Spine

Bones joined together

A long chain of bones runs down your back. It is called your spine, or backbone. It is made of 26 bones, called **vertebrae**, linked together so that you can twist and bend. Your backbone helps you to walk and run. It also protects the delicate nerves in your back. Your skull sits on the top two bones. The lowest bones are joined together, like a short tail.

AMAZING!

Even though it's the tallest animal in the world, a giraffe's neck has only seven bones, just like your neck!

Your muscles

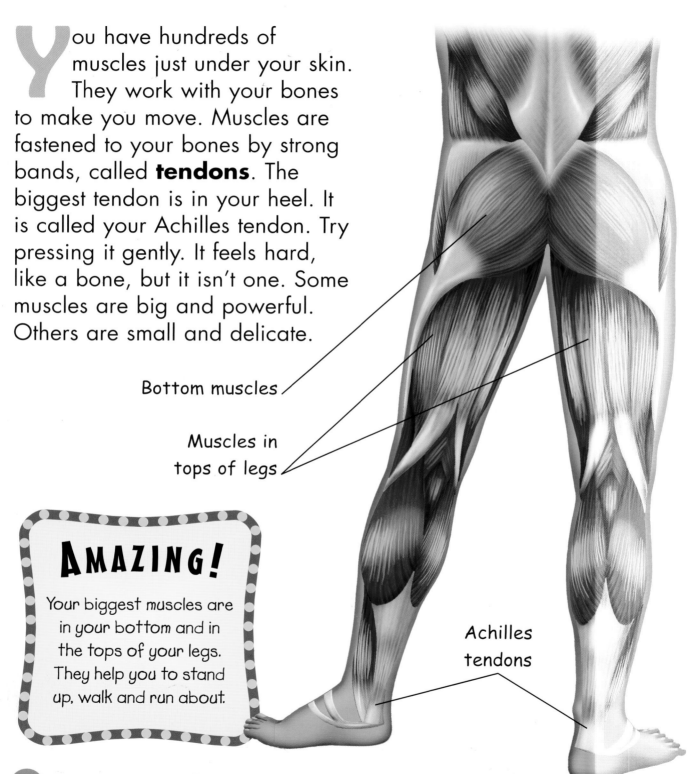

You have hundreds of muscles just under your skin. They work with your bones to make you move. Muscles are fastened to your bones by strong bands, called **tendons**. The biggest tendon is in your heel. It is called your Achilles tendon. Try pressing it gently. It feels hard, like a bone, but it isn't one. Some muscles are big and powerful. Others are small and delicate.

Bottom muscles

Muscles in tops of legs

Achilles tendons

AMAZING!

Your biggest muscles are in your bottom and in the tops of your legs. They help you to stand up, walk and run about.

Some muscles do not move bones. Muscles deep inside your body make your heart beat and your lungs breathe. Other muscles help you to **digest** your food. Tiny muscles in your face pull on your skin to make you smile or frown.

Muscles get bigger and stronger if you use them a lot. Many athletes train every day to make their muscles stronger.

LOOK AT ME! LOOK AT ME! LOOK AT ME! LOOK AT ME! LOOK AT ME! LOOK AT ME!

How big are your muscles? You can feel some of the muscles under your skin. Bend your arm and feel the top. This is your **biceps**.

Muscles at work

Muscles make you move by pulling on your bones. To make a bone move, a muscle gets shorter. This pulls on the bone and moves it. But muscles can only pull bones, not push them. So they often work in pairs. To move the bone back to where it was, another muscle gets shorter and pulls in the opposite direction.

AMAZING!

The smallest muscles are deep inside your ears. They pull on your tiny ear bones to stop loud sounds hurting your ears.

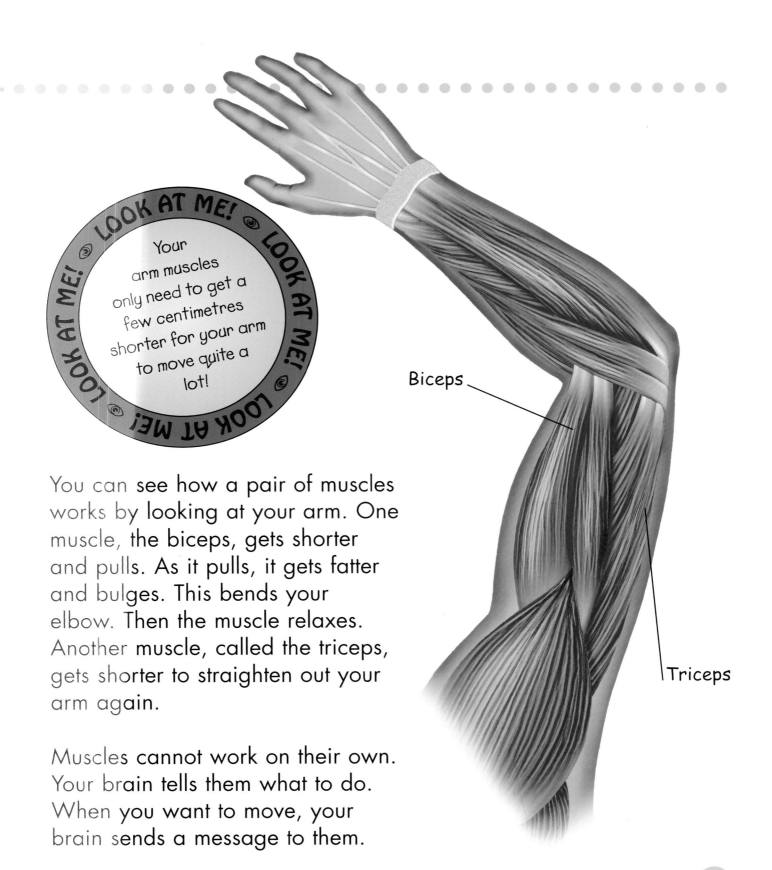

LOOK AT ME! ☺ LOOK AT ME! ☺ LOOK AT ME! ☺ LOOK AT ME! ☺

Your arm muscles only need to get a few centimetres shorter for your arm to move quite a lot!

Biceps

Triceps

You can see how a pair of muscles works by looking at your arm. One muscle, the biceps, gets shorter and pulls. As it pulls, it gets fatter and bulges. This bends your elbow. Then the muscle relaxes. Another muscle, called the triceps, gets shorter to straighten out your arm again.

Muscles cannot work on their own. Your brain tells them what to do. When you want to move, your brain sends a message to them.

Inside a muscle

Your muscles are made of very thin **fibres**, like tiny, stretchy elastic bands. Each of these fibres is made of even finer threads. When a muscle pulls, the fibres inside it get shorter. A stretchy skin around the muscle keeps it in shape.

AMAZING!

A big muscle, like the one in your leg, has hundreds of fibres inside it. Some fibres are up to 30 centimetres long.

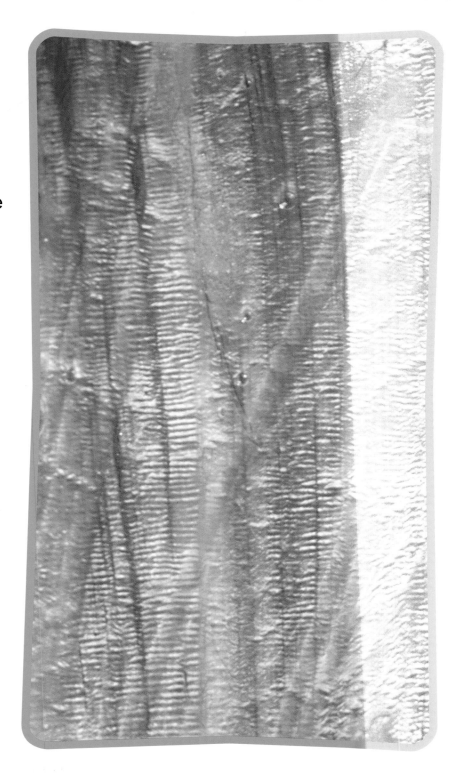

A muscle seen under a microscope. It shows the stretchy fibres.

Muscles need lots of energy to make them work. They get this from the food you eat and from the oxygen you breathe. Your blood carries the food and oxygen all over your body to your hard-working muscles.

Sometimes your muscles have to work hard but do not get enough energy. Then you might get **cramp**. This is when a muscle suddenly feels painful and tight. It feels like the muscle has got stuck. You need to stretch the muscle gently to stop it from hurting.

LOOK AT ME! @ LOOK AT ME! @ LOOK AT ME! @ LOOK AT ME!

Exercise is good for you! It helps keep your body healthy and strong. But stretch your muscles gently before you start to stop them from aching.

Hands and feet

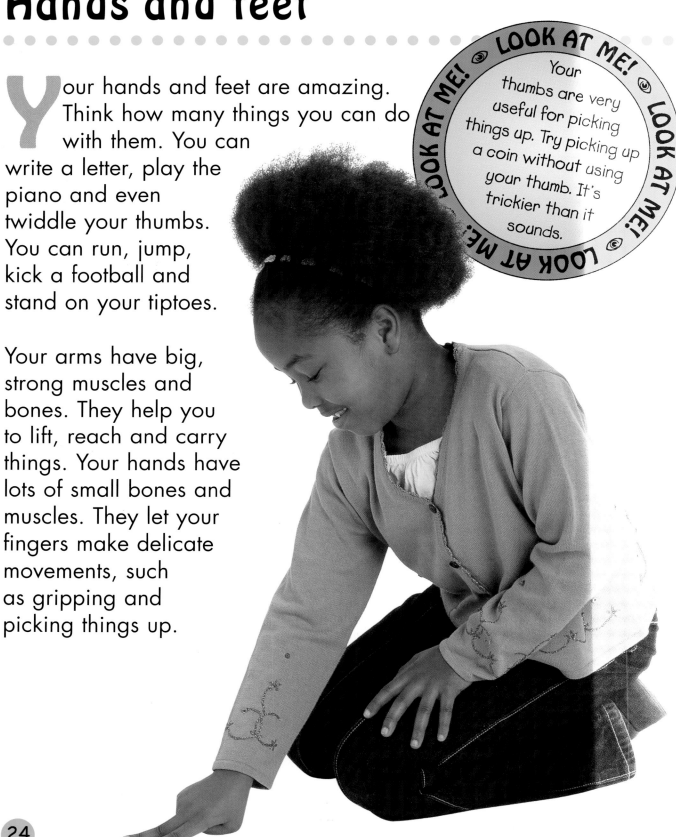

Your hands and feet are amazing. Think how many things you can do with them. You can write a letter, play the piano and even twiddle your thumbs. You can run, jump, kick a football and stand on your tiptoes.

Your arms have big, strong muscles and bones. They help you to lift, reach and carry things. Your hands have lots of small bones and muscles. They let your fingers make delicate movements, such as gripping and picking things up.

24

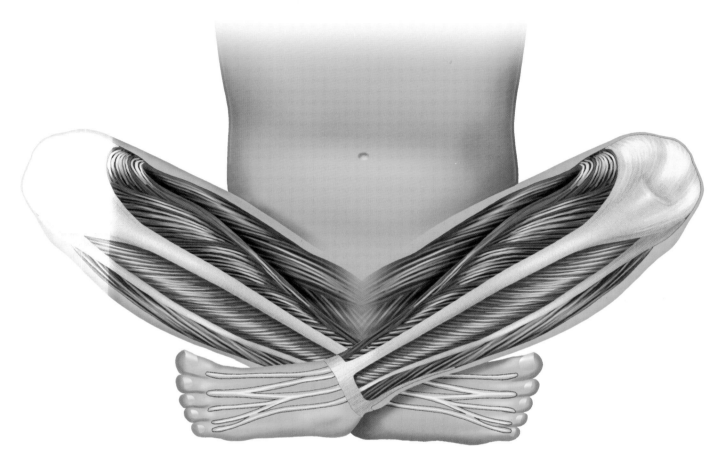

The long **muscles in your legs help you to sit cross-legged**.

AMAZING!

Your longest muscle runs down your leg from your hip to your knee.

Your legs and feet are built in a similar way to your arms and hands. Your legs are very long and strong. They support the weight of your body when you stand, walk and run. Walking uses lots of muscles from your bottom right down to your toes.

Funny faces

Look in a mirror and stick out your tongue. Now smile, then frown, then wrinkle up your nose. Every time you pull a face, you use lots of different muscles. These muscles do not move bones, like the muscles in your arms and legs. They pull on your skin to make your face move. Every muscle has a special job to do. When you smile, muscles in your cheeks pull up the corners of your mouth.

Forehead

Eyes

Nose

Lips

Neck

The main muscles in your face

AMAZING!

Are you ready for a surprise? You use about 50 different muscles when you pull a funny face.

You pull lots of funny faces every day. They help you to show other people how you are feeling. Are you feeling grumpy, happy or sad? All these faces are made by your muscles.

The busiest muscles in your face are those in your eyelids. They work very fast to make you blink thousands of times a day. Blinking covers your eyes with tears and helps to keep them clean and to protect them from harm.

27

Glossary

Biceps One of the sets of muscles in your upper arm. It pulls to bend your elbow.

Calcium An important substance that helps to build your bones and keep them strong.

Cells The tiny building blocks which make up every part of your body.

Cramp A sharp pain you feel when a muscle suddenly squeezes very tight.

Digest Break your food down into such tiny pieces that it can pass into your blood.

Fibres Very fine threads or bands.

Heart The large muscle in your chest which pumps blood around your body.

Joints The places where two bones meet up, such as your knees and shoulders. Joints allow you to move.

Ligaments Stretchy straps which hold the bones in a joint in place.

Lungs Two stretchy bag-like parts in your chest which fill with air as you breathe in, and empty as you breathe out.

Tendons Strong bands which attach your muscles to your bones. Your biggest tendons are in your heels. They are called your Achilles tendons.

Triceps One of the sets of muscles in your upper arm. It pulls to straighten your elbow.

Vertebrae The individual bones which link together to make up your spine, or backbone.

X-rays A special type of photograph used to look inside your body. Bones show up clearly in the picture.

Index